Want to make a warm wrap for yourself or one of your favorite friends or relatives, but don't have a lot of time? Then just get out your knitting needles and choose one of these fabulous throws which you can knit in a weekend.

Produced by
CREATIVE PARTNERS, LLC

Production Team
Pattern Testers: Kimberly Britt and Patricia Honaker
Technical Editor: Mary Ann Frits
Book Design: Linda Causee

Diagrams ©2018 by The Creative Partners, LLC Reproduced by special permission

Published by Leisure Arts, Inc.

LEISURE ARTS
the art of everyday living

10

12

14

16

18

20

22

WARM AND LACY

Finished Size: 35" x 56" (88.90 cm x 142.24 cm)

EASY

SHOPPING LIST

Yarn (Bulky Weight) 5

[3.5 ounces, 127 yards (100 grams, 116 meters) per skein]
8 skeins

Knitting Needles

36" (91.5 cm) circular
Size 11 (8 mm) or size required for gauge

Additional Supplies

Stitch markers
Large-eye yarn needle

GAUGE INFORMATION

In Garter Stitch (knit each row)
10 sts= 3" (7.62 cm)

Note: *Circular needle is used to accommodate large number of stitches. Do not join; work back and forth in rows.*

THROW INSTRUCTIONS

Cast on 117 sts loosely. Knit 2 rows; then work in pattern as follows.

Rows 1 through 4: Knit across.

Rows 5, 7, 9 and 11 (Right side): K5; *(K2 tog) twice; (YO, K1) 3 times; YO; (sl 1, K1, PSSO) twice, K1; rep from * to last 4 sts, K4.

Rows 6, 8, 10 and 12: K4, purl to last 4 sts, K4.

Repeat Rows 1 through 12 until the throw measures approximately 55" (139.70 cm) from CO edge, ending by working Row 12.

Knit 6 more rows. Bind off all sts loosely in knit. Weave in all ends.

BRIGHT AND BOLD

Finished Size: 35" x 56" (88.90 cm x 142.24 cm)

EASY

SHOPPING LIST

Yarn (Bulky Weight) 5

[12.7 ounces, 448 yards (360 grams, 410 meters) per skein]

Red (A) – 2 skeins

Grey (B) – 2 skeins

Knitting Needles

36" (91.5) circular

Size 11 (8 mm) or size required for gauge

GAUGE INFORMATION

In Stockinette Stitch (knit 1 row, purl 1 row)

14 sts = 4" (10 cm)

Note: *Circular needle is used to accommodate large number of stitches. Do not join; work back and forth in rows.*

STITCH GUIDE

Cluster (CL): P3tog, keeping 3 purl stitches on left-hand needle and transferring new stitch onto right-hand needle, YO, purl same stitches tog: 3 sts.

THROW INSTRUCTIONS

With Color A, CO 135 sts.

Carry unused color loosely along the side.

Row 1 (Right side): With Color A, knit across.

Row 2: With Color A, K1, P1; *CL, P1; rep from * to last st, K1.

Row 3: Join Color B, knit across.

Row 4: With Color B, K1, P3, CL; *P1, CL; rep from * to last 4 sts, P3, K1.

Repeat Rows 1 through 4 until the throw measures approximately 56" (142 cm) ending by working Row 4.

Last Row: With Color A, knit across.

Bind off all stitches loosely in knit. Weave in all ends.

FESTIVE LACE

Finished Size: 35" x 56" (88.90 cm x 142. 24 cm)

EASY

SHOPPING LIST

Yarn (Super Bulky) 6

[3.5 ounces, 127 yards (100 grams, 116 meters) per skein]
3 skeins

Knitting Needles

36" (91.5 cm) circular
Size 11 (8 mm) or size required for gauge

GAUGE INFORMATION

In pattern, 4 sts = 2" (5.08 cm)

Note: *Circular needle is used to accommodate large number of stitches. Do not join; work back and forth in rows.*

THROW INSTRUCTIONS

Cast on 75 sts loosely.

Row 1 (Wrong side): Purl across.

Row 2: K2; *YO, sl 1, K1, PSSO; K1, K2tog; YO, K1; rep from * across, ending last rep with K2 instead of K1.

Row 3: Purl across.

Row 4: K3; *YO, sl 1, K2tog, PSSO, YO, K3; rep from * across.

Rep Rows 1 through 4 until throw measures approx. 56" (142.24 cm) from CO edge, ending by working Row 1. Bind off all sts loosely in knit. Weave in all ends.

ENCHANTED LANDSCAPE

Finished Size: 36" x 56" (91.44 cm x 142.24 cm)

EASY

SHOPPING LIST

Yarn (Bulky Weight)

[3.5 ounces, 129 yards (100 grams, 118 meters) per skein]

8 skeins

Knitting Needles

36" (91.5 cm) circular
Size 10.5 (6.5 mm) or size required for gauge

GAUGE INFORMATION

In Stockinette Stitch (knit one row, purl one row)
12 sts = 4" (10 cm)

Note: *Circular needle is used to accommodate large number of stitches. Do not join; work back and forth in rows.*

THROW INSTRUCTIONS

Cast on 117 sts loosely.

Rows 1 through 4: Knit across.

Rows 5: K5; *(K2 tog) twice; (YO, K1) 3 times; YO, (sl 1, K1, PSSO) twice, K1; rep from * to last 4 sts, K4.

Row 6: K4, purl to last 4 sts, K4.

Row 7: Repeat Row 5.

Row 8: K4, purl to last 4 sts, K4.

Row 9: Repeat Row 5.

Row 10: K4, purl to last 4 sts, K4.

Row 11: Repeat Row 5.

Row 12: K4, purl to last 4 sts, K4.

Repeat Rows 1 through 12 until throw measures approximately 54" (137.16 cm). Knit 6 more rows. Bind off all sts loosely in knit. Weave in all ends.

SOPHISTICATION

Finished Size: 30" x 53" (76.20 cm x 134.62 cm)

EASY

SHOPPING LIST

Yarn (Bulky Weight) 5

[3.5 ounces, 127 yards (100 grams, 116 meters) per skein]

10 skeins

Knitting Needle

36" (91.5 cm) circular

Size 11 (8 mm) or size required for gauge

GAUGE INFORMATION

9 sts = 3" (7.62 cm)

Note: *Circular needle is used to accommodate large number of stitches. Do not join; work back and forth in rows.*

THROW INSTRUCTIONS

Cast on 113 sts.

Row 1 (Wrong side): Purl across.

Row 2: K2tog; *(K1, YO, K1) all in next st; sl 1 as if to purl, K2tog, PSSO; rep from * to last 3 sts; (K1, YO, K1) in next st; sl 1 as if to purl, K1, PSSO.

Repeat Rows 1 and 2 until throw measures approximately 53" (134.62 cm) from CO edge, ending by working Row 2.

Bind off all sts loosely in purl. Weave in all ends.

TRUE ELEGANCE

Finished Size: 43" x 43" (109.22 cm x 109.22 cm)

EASY

SHOPPING LIST

Yarn (Bulky Weight) 5

[6 ounces, 185 yards (170 grams, 169 meters) per skein]
4 skeins

Knitting Needle

36" (91.5 cm) circular
Size 11 (8 mm) or size required for gauge

Additional Supplies

10 stitch markers

GAUGE INFORMATION

In Garter Stitch (knit each row)
10 sts=3" (7.62 cm)

Note: *Circular needle is used to accommodate large number of stitches. Do not join; work back and forth in rows.*

Note: *Markers are used to indicate pattern repeats. Slip markers on each row.*

THROW INSTRUCTIONS

Cast on 108 sts. Knit 4 rows; then work in pattern as follows.

Row 1: Knit across.

Row 2: K4; *place marker, YO twice, K1; YO 3 times, K1; YO 4 times, K1; YO 3 times, K1; YO twice, K6; rep from * to last 4 sts, place marker, K4.

Row 3: Knit across, dropping all YO's from needle. (Gently tug on dropped sts so that they lie flat.) Slip markers.

Row 4: Knit, pulling on dropped sts across the row.

Row 5: Knit across.

Row 6: K4; *slip marker, K6, YO twice, K1; YO 3 times, K1; YO 4 times, K1; YO 3 times, K1; YO twice; rep from * to last 4 sts, K4.

Row 7: Knit across, dropping all YO's from needle. (Gently tug on dropped sts so that they lie flat.) Slip markers.

Row 8: Knit, pulling on dropped sts across the row.

Repeat Rows 1 through 8 until the throw measures approximately 43" (109.22 cm) from CO edge, ending by working Row 8.

Knit 4 rows. Bind off loosely in knit. Weave in all ends.

GORGEOUS GREEN

Finished Size: 30" x 60" (76.20 cm x 152.40 cm)

EASY

SHOPPING LIST

Yarn (Bulky Weight) 5
[4 ounces, 124 yards (113 grams, 113 meters) per skein]

7 skeins

Knitting Needle
36" (91.5 cm) circular
Size 11 (8 mm) or size required for gauge

GAUGE INFORMATION

In Garter Stitch (knit each row)
10 sts = 3½" (8.89 cm)

Note: *Circular needle is used to accommodate large number of stitches. Do not join; work back and forth in rows.*

THROW INSTRUCTIONS

Cast on 141 sts.

Row 1 (right side): K1; *YO, K3, P2, P3tog, P2, K3, YO, K1; rep from * across.

Row 2: P1; *P4, K5, P5; rep from * across.

Row 3: K1; *YO, K4, P1, P3tog, P1, K4, YO, K1; rep from * across.

Row 4: P1; *P5, K3, P6; rep from * across.

Row 5: K1; *YO, K5, P3tog, K5, YO, K1; rep from * across.

Row 6: P1; *P6, K1, P7; rep from * across.

Repeat Rows 1 through 6 until the work measures approximately 59" (149.86 cm) from CO edge, ending by working a Row 5. Bind off all stitches loosely in knit.

Weave in all ends.

WARM ALL

Finished Size: 36" x 56" (91.44 cm x 142.24 cm)

EASY

SHOPPING LIST

Yarn (Bulky Weight) 5

[3.5 ounces, 129 yards (100 grams, 118 meters) per skein]
7 skeins

Knitting Needle

36" (91.5 cm) circular
Size 11 (8 mm) or size required for gauge

GAUGE INFORMATION

In Garter Stitch (knit each row)
9 sts = 3" (7.62 cm)

Note: *Circular needle is used to accommodate large number of stitches. Do not join; work back and forth in rows.*

THROW INSTRUCTIONS

Cast on 112 stitches.

Rows 1 through 6: Knit across.

Row 7: Knit 5; *(P2tog) 3 times, (YO, K1) 5 times, YO, (P2tog) 3 times, rep from * to the last 5 stitches, K5.

Row 8: K5, P102, K5.

Row 9: Knit.

Row 10: K5, P102, K5.

Repeat Rows 7 through 10 until the throw is the desired size. Then, repeat Rows 1 through 6. Bind off all sts loosely in knit. Weave in all ends.

SENSATIONAL STRIPES

Finished Size: 36" x 56" (91.44 cm x 142.24 cm)

EASY

SHOPPING LIST

Yarn (Super Bulky) 6

[4.2 ounces, 80 yards (120 grams, 73 meters) per skein]

Dark - 8 skeins

Medium - 6 skeins

Light - 3 skeins

Knitting Needle

36" (91.5 cm) circular
Size 11 (8 mm) or size required for gauge

GAUGE INFORMATION

In Stockinette Stitch (knit 1 row, purl 1 row)

10 sts = 4" (10 cm)

Note: *Circular needle is used to accommodate large number of stitches. Do not join; work back and forth in rows.*

THROW INSTRUCTIONS

With Dark, cast on 90 sts.

Rows 1 through 6: With Dark, knit across.

Rows 7 and 8: With Medium, knit across.

Rows 9 through 12: With Dark, knit across.

Rows 13 and 14: With Light, knit across.

Rows 15 through 20: With Medium, knit across.

Rows 21 and 22: With Light, knit across.

Repeat Rows 1 through 22 until throw measures approximately 56" (142.24 cm). Repeat Rows 1 through 6. Bind off evenly across. Weave in all ends.

RAPID RIPPLE

Finished Size: 35" x 50" (88.9 cm x 127 cm)

EASY

SHOPPING LIST

Yarn (Bulky Weight)

[3.5 ounces, 127 yards (100 grams, 116 meters) per skein]
White (A) - 6 skeins
Black (B) - 2 skeins

Knitting Needle

36" (91.5 cm) circular
Size 13 (9 mm) or size required for gauge

GAUGE INFORMATION

In Garter Stitch (knit each row)
12 sts = 3.5" (8.89 cm)

Note: *Circular needle is used to accommodate large number of stitches. Do not join; work back and forth in rows.*

THROW INSTRUCTIONS

With Color A, cast on 126 sts loosely.

Row 1 (Right side): Knit across.

Row 2: Purl across.

Row 3: (K2tog) 3 times; *(YO, K1) 6 times, (K2tog) 6 times; rep from * to last 12 stitches, (YO, K1) 6 times, (K2tog) 3 times.

Row 4: Knit across.

Row 5: Knit across.

Row 6: Purl across.

Row 7: (K2tog) 3 times; *(YO, K1) 6 times, (K2tog) 6 times; rep from * to last 12 stitches, (YO, K1) 6 times, (K2tog) 3 times.

Row 8: Knit across.

Row 9: Knit across.

Instructions continued on page 24

Row 10: Purl across.

Row 11: (K2tog) 3 times; *(YO, K1) 6 times, (K2tog) 6 times; rep from * to last 12 stitches, (YO, K1) 6 times, (K2tog) 3 times.

Row 12: Knit across.

Row 13: Knit across.

Row 14: Purl across.

Row 15: (K2tog) 3 times; *(YO, K1) 6 times, (K2tog) 6 times; rep from * to last 12 stitches, (YO, K1) 6 times, (K2tog) 3 times.

Row 16: Knit across.

Row 17: Repeat Row 1.

Row 18: Purl across. At end of Row 18, cut Color A and attach Color B.

Row 19: With Color B, repeat Row 3.

Row 20: Repeat Row 4.

Row 21: Repeat Row 1.

Row 22: Repeat Row 2.

Row 23: Repeat Row 3.

Row 24: Repeat Row 4. At end of Row 24, cut Color B and attach Color A.

Repeat Rows 1 through 24 until Throw is desired length. Bind off loosely in knit. Weave in all ends.

YARN INFORMATION

Throws in this book were made using a variety of yarns. Any brand of the specified weight of yarn may be used. It is best to refer to yardage/meters when determining how many balls to purchase.

For your convenience, listed below are the specific yarns used to create our photography models. Because yarn manufacturers make frequent changes in the their product lines, you may sometimes find it necessary to use a substitute yarn or to search for the discontinued product at alternate suppliers (locally or online).

WARM AND LACY
Lion Brand® Lion's Pride® Woolspun®
#130 Honey

BRIGHT AND BOLD
Red Heart® Comfort Chunky®
Red - #4455 Claret (A)
Grey - #4468 Smoke (B)

FESTIVE LACE
Lion Brand ® Homespun® Thick & Quick®
#201 Coral Stripes

ENCHANTED LANDSCAPE
Red Heart® Infinity™
#9530 Enchanted

SOPHISTICATION
Lion Brand® Lion's Pride® Woolspun
#205 Quarry Print

TRUE ELEGANCE
Lion Brand® Homespun®
#429 Pueblo

GORGEOUS GREEN
Lion Brand® Wool-Ease® Tonal®
#171 Fern

WARM ALL
Red Heart® Infinity™
#9351 Almond

SENSATIONAL STRIPES
Bernat® Beyond™
Dark - #23002 Black
Medium - #23003 Slate
Light - #23004 Cream

RAPID RIPPLE
Lion Brand® Lion's Pride® Woolspun
Fisherman - #098 (A)
Black - #153 (B)

GENERAL INFORMATION

ABBREVIATIONS

Knitting instructions are written with many abbreviations which are used so that instructions don't take up too much space. They sometimes seem confusing, but once you learn them, you'll have no trouble following them.

Abbreviation	Meaning
BB	bobble
BO	bind off
CL	cluster
cm	centimeter
CO	cast on
DPN	double-pointed knitting needles
INC	increase(ing)
K	knit
Kfb	knit in front and back of same stitch
K2tog	knit two stitches together
M1	increase one stitch
mm	millimeter(s)
P	purl
P2tog	purl two stitches together
PSSO	pass the slipped stitch over
rem	remain(ing)
rep	repeat(ing)
rnd(s)	round(s)
sl	slip
sl st(s)	slip stitch(es)
SSK	slip, slip, knit
st(s)	stitch(es)
tog	together
YB	yarn in back of needle
YF	yarn in front of needle
YO	yarn over the needle

KNITTING TERMINOLOGY

The patterns in this book have been written using the knitting terminology that is used in the United States. Terms which may have different equivalents in other parts of the world are listed below:

United States	**International**
Gauge	Tension
Skip	Miss
Yarn over (YO)	Yarn forward (yfwd) or yarn around needle
Bind off	Cast off

GAUGE

Many knitters tend to shy away from "gauge" as if it were a dirty word. Gauge, however, is probably the most important word in a knitter's dictionary.

Gauge simply means the number of stitches per inch, and the number of rows per inch that result from a specific yarn worked with needles in a specific size. However, since everyone knits differently—some loosely, some tightly, some in between—the measurements of individual work can vary greatly, even when knitters use the same pattern, the same size needles, and the same size yarn.

The needle sizes given in any set of instructions are only guides. You should never go ahead with a project without making a small square to check your gauge. The knitter has the responsibility to make sure to achieve the gauge specified in the pattern. You may need to use a different sized needle from the one specified in the pattern. Actually the needle sizes given in instructions are just guides, and they never should be used without first making a gauge swatch.

Here's how you make a swatch to check your gauge. At the beginning of every knit pattern, you'll find a gauge such as the one given in the pattern on page 7 under Gauge Information. The pattern tells you that in stockinette stitch (knit one row, purl one row), 14 stitches will equal 4" (10 cm). The pattern has called for a size 11 (8 mm) knitting needle.

This actually means that you will work your gauge swatch in stockinette stitch and will try to achieve a gauge of 14 stitches to 4 inches. So cast on 14 stitches and work in stockinette stitch for at least 4" to adequately test your work.

If you have more stitches per inch than listed in the pattern, make another gauge swatch with larger size needles. If you have fewer stitches, make another swatch with smaller size needles.

Making gauge swatches before starting a project takes time, and it is a bother. But if you miss this important step, you'll never be able to create beautiful projects that fit perfectly.

STITCHES

Knit 2 stitches together (K2tog)

Insert the needle from left to right through the fronts of 2 stitches on the left needle and bring the yarn under and over the point of the needle.

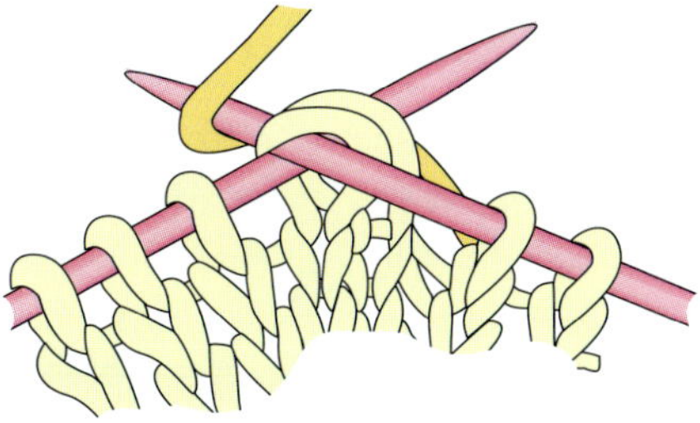

Draw the yarn through both stitches. Slip both stitches off the left needle, and one new stitch will be on the right needle. One stitch has been decreased.

Purl 2 stitches together (P2tog) Purl 3 stitches together (P3tog)

In much the same way, you can purl 2 or 3 stitches together. Insert the right hand needle from right to left through the fronts of 2 purl stitches on the left needle. Wrap the working yarn around as if you were purling one stitch.

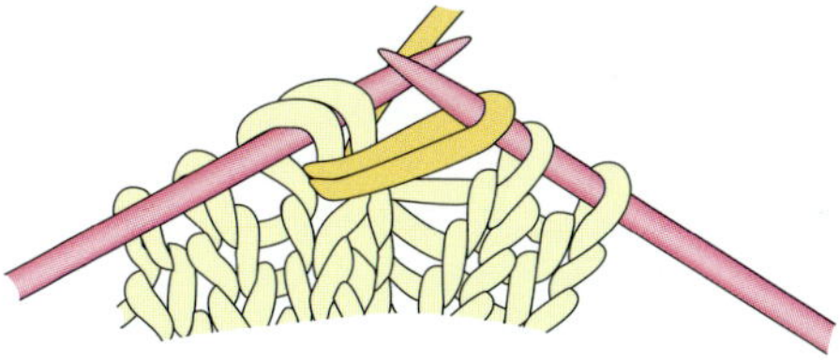

Slip (sl)

Slip the stitch from one needle to the other without working it. Insert the right needle into the stitch as if to purl (even if it is a knit stitch), but instead of actually purling, slip the stitch from the left needle to the right needle.

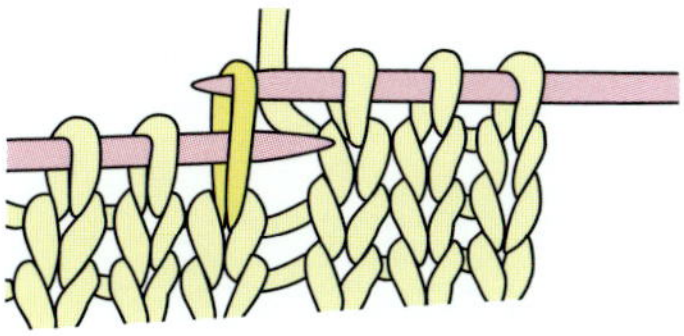

Yarn Over (YO)

Used to make an increase, the Yarn Over is basically just a loop of yarn that goes over the top of the working needle, moving first in front of the needle and then down in the back.

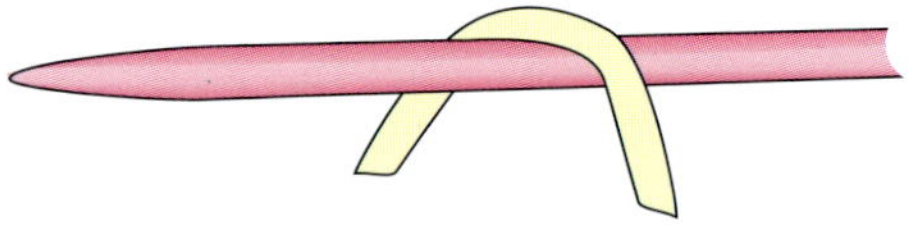

The stitch always begins with the yarn in front of the needle. For making a YO after a knit stitch, bring the yarn forward as if to purl, wrap the yarn over the needle and knit the next stitch.

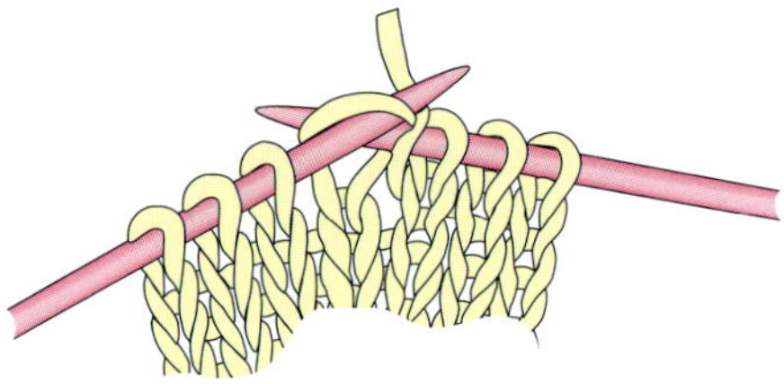

Slip, Slip, Knit (SSK)

Slip next two stitches, on at a time, as if to knit to the right needle.

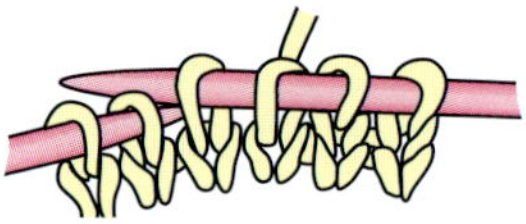

Insert left needle into fronts of these two stitches and knit them together.

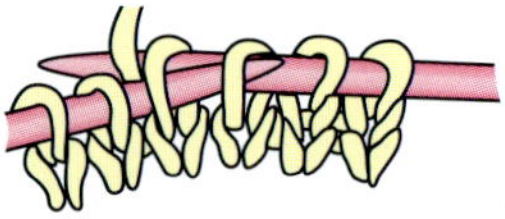

Pass the Slipped Stitch Over (PSSO)

Insert right needle, as if to knit, into the stitch, slip this stitch onto right-hand needle without knitting it, then knit the next stitch.

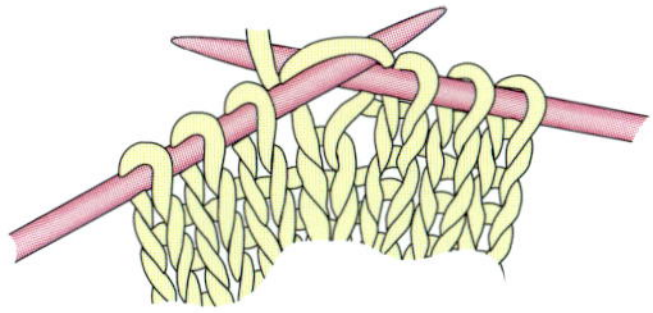

Using the left-hand needle, lift slipped stitch over the knit stitch and off the needle.

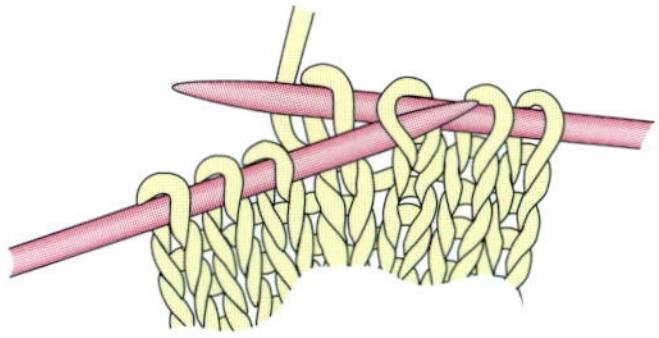

Slip 1, Knit 1, Pass Slipped Stitch Over (sl 1, K1, PSSO)

Slip one stitch as if to knit (Fig A), then knit the next stitch (Fig B). With the left needle, bring the slipped stitch over the knit stitch and off the needle.

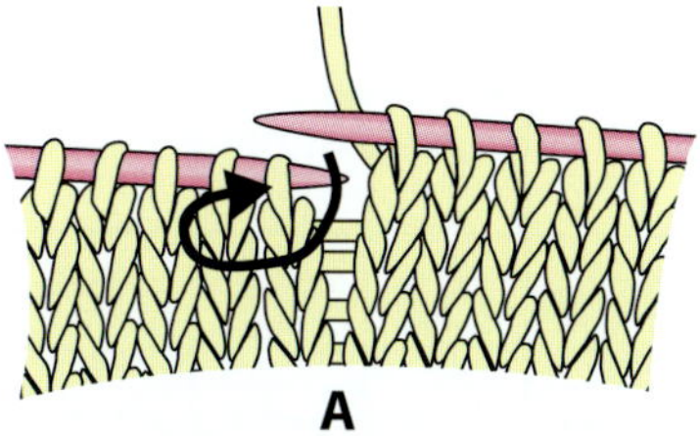

A

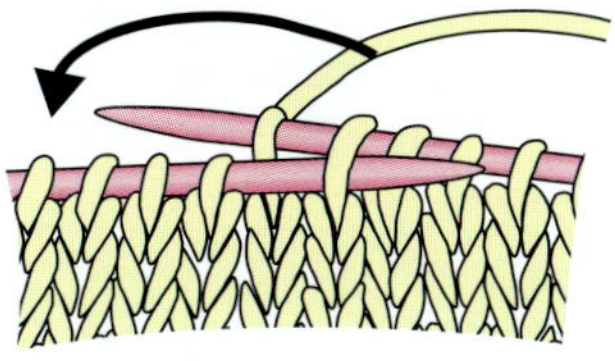

B

SKILL LEVELS

Yarn manufacturers, publishers, needle and hook manufacturers have worked together to set up a series of guidelines and symbols to bring uniformity to patterns. Before beginning a project, check to see if your skill level is equal to the one listed for the project.

	Beginner	Projects for first-time knitters using basic knit and purl stitches. Minimal shaping.
	Easy	Projects using basic stitches, repetitive stitch patterns, simple color changes, and simple shaping and finishing.
	Intermediate	Projects using a variety of stitches, such as basic cables and lace, simple intarsia, double-pointed needles and knitting in the round needle techniques, mid-level shaping and finishing.
	Experienced	Projects using advanced techniques and stitches, such as short rows, fair isle, more intricate intarsia, cables, lace patterns, and numerous color changes.

YARN WEIGHTS

To make it easier for yarn manufacturers, publishers, and designers to prepare consumer-friendly products and for consumers to select the right materials for a project, the following standard yarn weight system has been adopted.

Standard Yarn Weight System
Categories of yarn, gauge, ranges, and recommended needle and hook sizes

Yarn Weight Symbol & Category	0 Lace	1 Super Fine	2 Fine	3 Light	4 Medium	5 Bulky	6 Super Bulky	7 Jumbo
Type of Yarns in Category	Fingering 10 count crochet thread	Sock Fingering, Baby	Sport, Baby	DK, Light, Worsted	Worsted, Afghan, Aran	Chunky, Craft, Rug	Bulky, Roving	Jumbo, Roving
Knit Gauge Range* in Stockinette St itchto 4 inches	33-40** sts	27-32 sts	23-26 sts	21-24 sts	16-20 sts	12-15 sts	7-11 sts	6 sts and fewer
Recommended Needle in Metric Size Range	1.5-2.25mm	2.25-3.25mm	3.25-3.75mm	3.75-4.5mm	4.5-5.5mm	5.5-8mm	8-12.75mm	12.75mm and larger
Recommended Needle US Size Range	000 to 1	1 to 3	3 to 5	5 to 7	7 to 9	9 to 11	11 to 17	17 and larger

* **GUIDELINES ONLY:** The above reflect the most commonly used gauges and needle sizes for specific yarn categories.
** Lace weight yarns are usually knitted on larger needles to create lacy, openwork patterns. Accordingly, a gauge range is difficult to determine. Always follow the gauge stated in your pattern.

Made in U.S.A.